HOW TO MAKE A WOMAN HAPPY

A MEN'S GUIDE TO CONJUGAL BLISS

BY

CORNELIUS WHITNEY HYZER, SR.

ISBN 978-0-557-02432-2

DEDICATION

This book is dedicated to my dear wife

with all my love.

SUCCESS IN THE HOME CAN COMPENSATE

FOR ANY OTHER FAILURE

INTRODUCTION

This book is **not** how to make all women happy but rather the **one** special woman that a man chooses to marry and make happy all of her life. A wise man once said, "I can make all women happy," but he became a fool when he tried to prove it. Life is too short to make ridiculous goals, but making one woman happy can make all the difference.

Because readers will be at different stages of life, this book is arranged in helpful chapters that may be read as individual needs vary. In other words, skip around and use what looks like it might work. Hopefully some readers will be young enough or perhaps at a point of a new beginning where the entire book will prove useful. More experienced relationships will benefit from some chapters but not others. This is to be expected.

Obviously, I do not have all the answers. I only have suggestions and lessons learned, some positive and some negative. I do promise that these experiences are all true, which makes them easier to remember and more fun to relate, but they are from my perspective and not my wife's!

I offer this as a guide to men, but understanding the curiosity of women when it comes to the male psyche, I have not fully expressed myself in a manner where only men would be "in the room," so to speak. If the reader does not know what I am talking about, it would not be possible to explain further. But those who do will understand that sometimes things are expressed openly and frankly by men, for which they later pay a heavy price. It is not good to be a bull in a china closet, and this book is definitely full of china.

On a more somber note, our modern American society is cannibalizing itself, and needs all the help it can get to restore fabric that is quickly molding and full of decay. There is no "quick fix." That which has seen 100 years of decline will take even longer to improve, and with the rapid technological and social changes we see taking place all around us, it cannot be imagined where our society will be 100 years from now. However, people are still people, and men and women will still seek personal fulfillment in their lives as friends and lovers, husbands and wives, and hopefully children will still need loving parents to show them the ways of life and happiness.

That's what this book is all about.

Cornelius W. Hyzer, Sr.
October 2015

INDEX

CHAPTER ONE

COURTING

Courting is serious dating. This is not high school stuff. When a man gets serious about life, it is time to find the future mother of his children, the love of his life, the partner of his dreams, the queen for his castle. The first thing necessary to make a woman happy is to court a virgin. This can be literal, or figurative. Unfortunately, in our modern society, "figuratively" is more likely, but "literal" is still possible. If you find a virgin, keep her that way until after the preacher says, "I now pronounce you Husband and Wife!" If she is less than literally a virgin, it is crucial for her future happiness, and yours, of course, that her virtue and virginity be considered restored as to your relationship, and scrupulously maintained! (Should I not neglect to mention that *your* virginity may be somewhat tarnished and in need of restoration as well?)

I cannot emphasize this enough. We are talking about the next 50 years of your happiness in life, so the foundation of your house of happiness must be solid as granite! One slip and the memory will never go away! Make fidelity in the courtship your highest priority. I am talking about no premarital sex, including petting. Make her body a temple and you are the temple guard. Make her the castle you will die defending and be her moat. Save the good-times for the honeymoon, and the next several decades will be far happier with the love of your life, with the memory of a courtship that was honorable. You will need your wife's trust and respect in the future, so that must be cultivated in the courting period.

I was 24 when I married my sweetheart and she was 23. We had known each other over 2 years. When I was in the Navy, I met an old guy and I complained that the girls in the bars were hardly worth dating. He told me that if I wanted to meet a good girl to date, I should go to church. I never laughed so hard! I could just imagine myself going to church to get a girlfriend. Over a year later after I had a "spiritual awakening" and became a Bible reading church-goer, I noticed that there were some pretty young women there. Unfortunately, none of them would go out with me. Only after many months did I have a chance to talk to one or two long enough to be invited over for dinner. I began to realize that this could take some time.

I met my future wife at a conservative university in the fall and only talked to her briefly the first few months. We really did not "hit it off." Her roommate liked me and that made me "off limits" in my future bride's thinking. Sometimes you have to network. When I got a new roommate in January, her roommate became interested in him instead of me. That development made me "available" and my future bride began to develop feelings for me. (Naturally, I did not know any of this until later!)

Take mental notes of likes and dislikes to use to your advantage at a future moment! I learned that she was interested in reading, and bought Christmas presents for her and her roommates, not trying to single her out, but the book I bought for her showed her that I was listening. This impressed her and it is a fond memory for her to this day! It makes her happy every time she sees that book on our bookshelf.

My wife teases me to this day that we never went on a "date" when I knew her in college. I just kept hanging around. I mention this because money was not an issue. She was the cheapest girlfriend I ever had. All I had to do was go over to her apartment and say "Hi." We liked to talk and to be together. We did go on a group date before we started to get serious. We saw "The Ten Commandments." Unfortunately I tried to put my arm around her and she thought I was "fresh." To

-15-

this day, I really don't know what that means.
Anyway, I had to apologize and was greatly
embarrassed. There were witnesses and socially it
was a disaster for me. The only good that came
from it was that she knew I liked her. So I guess I
went out on a limb, got the limb cut off, but landed
on my feet. Sometimes I say really stupid things.

I knew I was making progress when she
asked me to meet her family for dinner. I had
already told her that I dated a lot in the Navy. So
when her grandfather warned her about the "past"
of a Navy man, she was able to tell him that I had
already mentioned my past sinful ways, and this
impressed him. Candor is always good. Her father
wondered how she managed to find a "decent guy"
for a change. They did not always approve of the
young men she brought home, but I was given the
"OK!"

As part of the "family interview" they
wanted to know my career goals. I told them that I
wanted to be a lawyer. This was a goal I had had
from high school. It was the truth. They were
impressed, but in hindsight, I think they should have
thrown me out the door! I was only in my first year
of college! But they bought it and the experience is
a fond memory.

When looking for a good future wife,
beware of riches. My wife came from a
hardworking humble home. She drove a vintage car

that did not make it through that first winter I knew her. She worked at a job making minimum wage, for a boss that would have made Scrooge proud. The first five years of our marriage were college years, with little money, living on the GI Bill, and in low rent apartments. They are wonderful memories.

Learn how to play chess. Let your future bride know in your own way that you have some brains and that you will use them to make her life happy. Write in a journal your daily activities and mention her while you are courting her. I have references in my journal from those fun courting days that "prove" to her that I was thinking seriously about her long before I ever made my feelings known to her.

March 31st was the first kiss. I was showing her some chess moves, and somehow she ended up sitting on my lap with my arms around her. I think she was putting the moves on me, but I did not suspect a thing. Then she hit me hard with the question, "You're afraid to kiss me, aren't you?" I had known her over 6 months by that time and earlier promised myself that the next girl I kissed I would marry. I already knew enough about kissing so I didn't need the practice. So I kissed her, while promising in my mind that this was the woman I was going to marry! It was a long kiss and she didn't breathe--she almost passed out! It was a kiss she'll never forget! We never did finish that chess game.

Make your courting time as memory-filled as possible. Her white dress on her wedding day should mean what it symbolizes. It did for my wife and that has made my woman very happy.

Years later, my wife told me that at some point in our courtship we went to a café and I tipped the waitress with what my wife thought was a generous tip. I'm sure it was just a dollar or two, when a quarter would have sufficed. My wife told me that when she was a waitress, she appreciated a decent tip. It was an indication to her early on that I was a decent guy. She also mentioned that in her waitressing days, an older man brazenly asked her to be his mistress. She was shocked into silence. Her manager overheard the man's rudeness, and quickly responded, "You can't afford her!" He was so right. A good wife and mother costs everything you have and more. You have to give her your heart and dedicate your life to making her happy.

I proposed to her "on bended knee" on a hilltop overlooking the city, and she accepted. I had no money for a diamond ring, but showed her the two simple gold bands I had purchased, one for her and one for me. It was over 10 years later before I bought her a diamond ring, but it was a great memory when it finally happened.

Courtship ends the day of the wedding. Many say you should continue courting into the marriage, but I discovered marriage is profoundly different. As we drove away after the reception, in my brother's Corvair, (I didn't own a car when we got married), the awesome responsibility of being her husband began to dawn on me. She was placing her whole life in my incompetent hands. She had to be crazy. I looked into her eyes and saw the trust and love she had for me; that I would protect her, provide for her, and love her for the rest of my life. Being married should be "uber" courting.

While driving across Texas as part of our honeymoon, she wanted to stop for breakfast. I thought the cheese and crackers in the car should hold us over until a stop at lunch time. This was when I learn my first lesson about marriage. What she wants, she gets. She was hungry and she wanted food now. So "we" stopped for breakfast. She thought I was mad because I did not order any. She was much happier as she ate, and I relented somewhat, eating some of her food that she did not want. We got back into the car, and I had learned an important lesson. Obedience brings happiness. However, forty years later, she told me the rest of the story. She had never eaten breakfast in a restaurant before in her whole life, and she wanted it to be a new experience as part of our honeymoon. I had no idea. Forty years later, she is still mad at me for being a goof!

A HAPPY MEMORY!

CHAPTER 2

FLOWERS

When I was a young man, I learned very quickly that potted plants don't work. This is a female idiosyncrasy. The proper flower gift has to be freshly cut, or as I call them, "dead flowers." I never have figured this out. The other important thing is to make flower giving sporadic. If flowers become a symbol of atonement, an admission of guilt, or a gesture of asking forgiveness, you are in trouble. They should only be a symbol of love and joy and thus far more innocuous and less likely to imply that other things are going on. If flowers show up only in times of trouble, then when you want to give them for the fun of it, she will think there is trouble. This goes for candy and other gifts as well.

However, it is mandatory that flowers be present at the hospital when she gives you a son or a daughter. New motherhood must have flowers, even if the funds restrict you to $5. As they say, it is the thought that counts. If you forget to bring flowers on the first visit after the baby is born, you are toast. There will be no fond memory. We had eight children and I always brought flowers. (I tried a potted plant the first time and learned quickly that that did not count.)

Flowers given while courting can be tricky because of the money question, timing, and what to do next time. You will also fall into the comparison with other guys who brought flowers in the past. Flowers presented at the moment of the formal marriage proposal can work very nicely, but I never gave flowers until after we were married. Do what you think is best; especially if she gives you a hint on the subject, but I seriously doubt you will ever hear her say, "Gee, I have always wanted the practical gift of a potted plant!" (except for my daughter-in-law; you just never know for sure with women!).

This subject deserves its own chapter because flowers are a big deal to women. I have no clue why a dozen long-stemmed red roses move them so much. It is a very powerful weapon to be used sparingly, something like a "daisy bomb." To use it on a first date could backfire on several levels. What do you give her on the second date?

So it may be wiser to start small and build. The cost is also a factor since this stuff can get expensive. A lady does not get impressed with expensive gifts. She actually thinks that someone is try to "buy" her. She is not for sale. I took a lot of dates to expensive restaurants in my younger years and the results were disappointing. Of course there was only one result I was looking for, but I overlooked the "Not For Sale" sign on many occasions.

Candy as a gift is very dangerous. Young women are greatly concerned about their weight and skin conditions. Before going out on that limb, a thorough recon is necessary. You have to consider the kind of nuts, flavors, and types of chocolate. After more than 40 years of marriage, I am finally safe in giving chocolates, but no matter what, be sure to give your true love a box of chocolates on Valentine's Day. Miss that one and you will never hear the end of it! Flowers and candy can also be effective on anniversaries and birthdays.

CHAPTER 3

MARRIAGE

Marriage is a big deal. When we got married I figured a few quick words and we should be off on the Honeymoon! Yahoo! But I was wrong. I did not see the need for a tuxedo at the big reception. I was wrong again. Over the years and countless weddings of family and friends, I have learned that marriage is a BIG deal; especially to women. So plan on a big wedding and the bigger the better! Make her really happy! The public celebration of the union of a man and a woman to begin a new family unit, designed by God to raise children, brings a community together. The public announcement in the newspaper with invitations all printed up and mailed to family and friends makes it clear that something important is taking place. It really is the formal commitment of two people to become one, in order to propagate the species, to build the next generation of our society. To be able to share in that event is a great privilege.

As a member of a small church in Wisconsin during my first years as a lawyer, I was authorized to perform weddings. I performed only two marriages but I experienced the societal wisdom of solemnizing such unions and learned to appreciate the goodness of the institution of marriage. I deeply regretted doing the paperwork for divorces. My old law professor said "never bury a live marriage because it will come back." So my first question of a divorce client was always, "Do you still love him [or her]?" If the answer was "yes" then I would help my client become reconciled. It did not always work, but I sincerely tried.

One time my client said "yes" and I suggested he take her flowers and candy, as a token of his love and desire to be forgiven. A few days later he returned and said it didn't work. I asked him how it went. He said, "I knocked on the door and said to her, 'Here are your d___ flowers and your d___ candy!' and she threw them back at me!" I agreed with him that it was time to get the paperwork started on his divorce.

Some time ago, I was helping decorate the church for a wedding reception and began to talk to the aunt of the bride. She mentioned that she herself would soon remarry. I asked if she was going to use a justice of the peace and she said emphatically that it was going to be a big wedding this time, not small and quick like her first one.

It is always nice to remember that Adam and Eve were married in the Garden of Eden before they ate the forbidden fruit, (See Genesis 2:25 "the man and his wife"), "and not ashamed."

The joy of newlyweds cannot be measured. The memories will last the rest of their lives. A small, quick wedding does not produce an abundance of happy memories for a woman.

CHAPTER 4

CHILDREN

Once married, babies became the key to my wife being very happy. So we had lots of them. My grandmother always said, "The first one can come anytime, but the rest take nine months." Our first one took ten months.

We had another baby about every two years, and later in our marriage the spacing was longer. Seven boys came first and our last baby was our precious daughter. Food was important and I followed my father's advice which was to buy lots of potatoes. We dug a fruit cellar at our ranch and filled it with potatoes each fall. To this day my boys love to have potato soup when they come to visit.

To keep things in balance, we told our children that we were the parents and they were the children. It works nicely that way. To maintain some order in the midst of chaos, I would try to support my wife in her decisions concerning the children. "Stabbing [her] in the back," as she called it, was not helpful to our marriage relationship. As a family, we (meaning my seven boys and I) recognized that Mom had full veto power like one of the permanent members of the UN Security Council. In other words, our combined 8 votes in favor would always lose to her 1 vote against. This made her happy and us sad. We got over it.

One job that fell directly on me was the duty of sex education. Naturally, I skillfully avoided it. Unfortunately, the time always came, as each boy grew older, when my dear wife would order me into the bedroom to council a young lad on the proper time and usage of various body parts. I would humbly consent to this requirement of fatherhood and enter the room where the innocent victim awaited the most important talk of his life with his dad. My first question was always, "You already know everything, right?" and the answer was either, "Of course, dad" or the smart aleck "What questions do you have, dad?" So with that out of the way, we would talk about the latest camping trip or plan our next outing to kill a half-hour, and then proudly leave the room. Usually my all-wise wife would say, "You didn't tell him anything, did you?"

I firmly believe some things should best be left un-discussed. Sex is definitely number 1 on that list. The less children know about it the better for everyone. They will figure it out once they are married. Girls need to learn some details from their mothers, but those monthly problems are definitely none of my business, and as long as I am on this subject, it was always highly embarrassing to me to have to buy certain paper products at the store in the middle of the night because somebody forgot to. I am *not* talking about paper diapers.

My father's advice to me as a young man concerning girls was simply, "Keep your pants on." I did not know what he was talking about at the time and only wondered if it was OK to take off my shirt. I did not understand why I would be doing anything with my clothes if I was taking a young woman on a date to dinner and a movie. Later in life I understood more and also noticed other young men who could have used my father's advice to their advantage. I had some interesting paternity and custody cases while practicing family law.   I saw many situations where lots of problems could have been avoided, if they had just "kept their pants on."

Sometimes our children would play the sneaky game of "Mom said it would be OK if you said OK" only to find out later that Mom said "No." They were working "both sides of the street." This brought swift retribution from both Mom and Dad. We spanked the kids more in the early years and the last several children hardly got spanked at all. The older boys thought the younger ones should be spanked more and unilaterally undertook that duty. Things got pretty rough sometimes raising seven boys, akin to nuclear war, but nobody ever had to go to the hospital. Sometimes a wall or a piece of furniture had to be repaired. Controlling these battles was my job, as my dear wife would inform me, not hers. Sometimes you just have to let these storms "blow themselves out."

Now that most of our children are married and gone, the grandbabies are our greatest joy and source of happiness. I heard of a father with older unmarried daughters comment that he was so desperate for grandbabies that he told his daughters at this point marriage was optional! Our married sons have achieved happy marriages primarily by just following our example. At a recent wedding reception, a little boy asked his dad, "Why did they all marry such beautiful women?" His father replied, "I don't know; you'll have to ask them." These fruits of a successful marriage have made my wife very happy.

If you and your wife are unable to have children naturally, then adopt. There are plenty of children out there who need a home with love in it. I was privileged to be the attorney for many adoptions and step-parent adoptions. Every time the judge involved would say how much joy there was in doing adoption cases in contrast to the usual cases that came into the courtroom. The sense of societal healing was always present.

We need more adoptions.

We were blessed with poverty, I always said. This made raising our children much easier. When we said we could not afford something, the boys knew we were not kidding. We lived on our ranch over seven years, while most of the boys were in their teens. They learned how to fix cars, drive a clutch, and haul water. We lived "off the grid." That meant using generators and inverters with batteries or running the car to watch a movie with the VCR. A 12-volt demand-pump ran the water system in the house. We purchased on credit a propane refrigerator which gave us ice in the summer with its small freezer, and my brother-in-law gave us a wood stove. The mobile home on the ranch was small, so we built an 8'x 8' addition and put the sofa, TV, and the wood stove in it. The older boys slept in the old truck camper (sans truck), with a kerosene heater to keep them warm. It was quite old and full of holes so venting was not a problem. I drove truck for a local outfit about twenty miles from the house, but the interstate rest area was available on the trip home every day, so I could fill up the water barrel in the trunk of my car. The water hose from the house fit nicely in the top and the 12-volt pump would pressurize the pipes and propane hot water system.

By the time we left the ranch we had our own water well, two pumps (a 220 volt and a 12 volt), a wind generator, deep-cycle batteries, a big inverter that could run the washing machine, a 400 gallon fresh water holding tank, a 5 bedroom, 1 ½ bathroom, triple-wide, with a 20' x 16' family room and solar panels. Our last generator was an air-cooled 10-kw diesel. We also had a trampoline and an above ground swimming pool.

Things did improve over time. Our children learned to care for animals, get by without, and sleep in a cold bedroom. The boys started baling hay for a local rancher when they were 14. They learned how to manage their money and that "loaning" money to dad was more like a gift to be given ungrudgingly. I did feed them in return. They got married and went to college.

One day my wife and our youngest son were standing in the parking lot at Wal-mart, when he said to her pointing to houses on a nearby hill, "Wouldn't it be great if we could live in one of those houses?" My wife laughed. Less than a month later we moved in to one of those houses, thanks to a school-teacher friend whose neighbor was about to lose his house to the bank. I would not have made it without some truly great friends. But my best friend is my wife.

CHAPTER 5

CAREER CHANGES

Life has many exciting moments to enjoy and changing jobs is not one of them. After practicing law for over 10 years, it was time for a change. This was obvious because we could not pay the rent and the government was paying for our last baby. I had several clients who were truck drivers and they were bringing in more money than I was. So with their help, I studied for my commercial driver's license and passed the written test. Armed with a student permit, one owner-operator took pity on me and after a month of team driving, we found a private tester, paid $50.00 cash money, and I passed my road test. I had a CDL. The fact that I could not drive an 18-wheeler did not stop me from applying for jobs as a truck driver. My new goal was to learn the trucking business and start my own trucking company. Yeah.

Anyway, after three months of long-haul driving with a company on the verge of bankruptcy (i.e., they were desperate for drivers), my wife informed me that she would no longer take care of the eight children without me home so I must either get a local driving job or a divorce. I chose the local driving job. It took six months to find a decent paying local driving job. This was one of those situations where we were so broke that bankruptcy was not necessary. In fact, we never did file bankruptcy from that point forward, although we had in the past. However, my long-haul job did give me enough experience that I was able to move forward in my new career, and eventually became senior driver at a chemical transportation terminal. We bought a 20 acre ranch and had horses, chickens, and a bunch of other critters! The children grew up and some got married while we lived on our ranch over the next 7 years.

After switching jobs to a different trucking company (hauling diesel and gasoline), we moved into town and bought a house. My next career change came because my wife wanted me to have a permanent steady job at a local goldmine. She talked to the head of their human resources department one day, whom she had met since we moved into town, and got me the job. She was so tired of me driving truck and working all hours of the day and weekends, that she was determined that I should take this new position. I wisely accepted.

After that when I worked overtime, she could not complain, and our finances steadily improved. When I worked December 24th, she did not complain because I was getting double-time and a half pay for my 11 ½ hour shift. Our marital bliss has increased greatly since complaints about my work schedule have ceased. I miss truck driving, but my first assignment at the goldmine was to drive the 85 ton water truck! In the winter, when water generally freezes, I was assigned the job of pulling steel out of the ore in the crusher, but moved into a loader, and part-time yard tractor operator moving trailers to be unloaded. I was back in an 18-wheeler several times a week!

Being flexible in career choices and keeping a positive attitude can make this part of life an adventure for both you and your wife. I have been an owner-operator, a terminal manager, and as part of my legal profession, a tax collector, a public defender, an insurance claims adjuster, disability examiner with Social Security, and an administrative law hearing officer for the government. My wife has also had several jobs. This has really helped out, especially when we had car payments to make.

All these career changes had various effects on my wife's level of happiness. I will say that she was always happier when I could work closer to home and make enough money to pay the bills. I hope you have better luck than I had! My final suggestion is that lots of "pillow talk" late at night can ease the transitions. Once you are both on the same page, whatever happens, you are in it together. You can grow closer together from these experiences. One part of life is the unexpected, so share it with your best friend and business partner, your wife!

CHAPTER 6

THE NEW TRUCK

Many a new marriage has hit the first bumps on the road of life when money enters the picture. This can become the greatest source of conflict in a marriage. Everything else can be wonderful and perfect, but when finances go sour, so does the marriage. It is a popular belief that most divorces are caused by financial problems. As a divorce lawyer for over 10 years, I found that a lack of forgiveness and loss of love were the primary reasons, but financial problems were definitely a huge contributing factor.

A few suggestions in this area of grave concern are:

1. Have separate checking accounts. They can be "joint" to avoid probate in the event of a death in the family, and each

spouse should be open about the use of their individual funds. Bills may be allocated and taxes filed jointly. For many years my wife stayed home raising the children, so we experimented with her paying the bills while I was off on business trips. Later, she had direct deposit into her account, while my check went into my account. We have tried successfully many saving programs and retirement plans. We bought homes and filed bankruptcy. Our finances have been truly amazing. My wife would use a different word. For her own reasons, she no longer opens the mail. That has been good for me, and has promoted marital harmony.

2. <u>Use credit cards sparingly</u>. This is great advice we plan to follow someday.

3. <u>Don't get a second mortgage</u>. This is also great advice. No further comment is necessary.

4. <u>Beware of business partners or get rich quick ideas, because they *NEVER* work out</u>. Abraham Lincoln started out in a retail business with a partner who was a drunk and decided to go into law to pay off the resulting debt. Before he left town, however, the sheriff sold his horse to satisfy one creditor, so he had to walk to Springfield. He did not have a wife to warn him ahead of time!

My partner was a drunk and a druggie, so when the money disappeared, it was a lot and went quickly. Because I did some quick damage control, the Bar Association only issued a "letter reprimand" but I still had to pay the money back. Jail was suggested, but I also did some criminal law and knew the prosecutors would rather have the publicity of putting me in jail, rather than some paralegal. So I prudently forgave, rather than face a trial over who said what, where no matter what I said, I was the lawyer and should have known better. And I should have known better. My wife was right. Admitting this sort of thing promotes marital bliss. Wives love it when men admit they really blew it! (Anyway, you won't believe what the IRS did to my ex-partner 3 years later when I was audited and the IRS agent helped me file an amended return with a 1099 deduction on my Schedule C!)

Every time this episode in our marriage comes up, I just confess how right she was and she gets this warm, happy feeling of knowing she was right and I was stupid for not listening to her in the first place. Thus I wisely turned a horrible disaster into a happy memory for her every time it comes up.

5. <u>Make your wife the final decision-maker on important purchases</u>. This is only logical since it is harder to hide major

purchases, like a house or a new truck. If she has the final say, then you will be safe in assuming that she will help pay for it. Hopefully she will be willing to sacrifice other things, like food, if the family budget gets a little tight because you are out-of-budget by, say $500.00 per month.

For over 25 years we never had a car payment. We did not have a decent car either. My sons and I worked on cars constantly trying to keep something on the road to go to church, school, work, and the grocery store. One day the radio ad said no one would be turned down, just come on in and apply for credit. I immediately called my wife on my cell phone from my big truck and she went to the dealer. Two hours later she called me and said I was approved for a car loan. $5,000 seemed like a lot, but with $500 down, we had a nice used car; a Saturn, with only 30,000 miles on it. Six weeks later, on Easter Sunday, my sweet and greatly loved wife was driving alone through a local intersection and got hit by a pickup truck on the passenger side. Naturally, I was greatly concerned for her safety and welfare. I did not have a seconds thought about my new car. I could have killed her, but there was no financial benefit to that, although I would have felt better. Forgiveness is such a virtue. I guess I had more of it in me than I thought.

It took six weeks for the insurance company to decide it was not a "total" and to get it fixed. The boys in the auto shop literally rebuilt the car and gave back to me a "new" car. It was a very happy day, and my wife went with me to pick it up.

My deductible was $500 so I wrote them a "bad" check figuring the utility bills could wait a couple of weeks. I had to take the insurance check to the dealer to sign due to the lien on the car, and return the check to the auto shop. While leaving the dealer, our salesman from 6 weeks earlier asked, "Is there anything else we can help you with?" My quick smart answer was, "Yea, loan me $1,000 bucks!" to which he replied, "I can do better than that. I can sell you a brand new car and put the $1,000 cash rebate in your pocket." I said, "Show me the car." I drove the Saturn back to the auto shop to drop off the check and my wife drove her new car home. I figured if she was going to get into another car wreck, at least it should be her car she wrecks, and not mine!

Two years later: Perhaps not the best way to buy a pickup truck.

This part of the story may not sound too good. After refinancing the house for the 4th time and moving the new car loan on to the house, I was impressed by the latest flyer from our friendly car dealer, indicating an end of the year massive rebate deal on trade-ins. So, things being the way they were, (yes, we were broke again), I drove my Saturn (lien balance of $4,800) to the car dealer and bought a new used car, a Grand Prix, with 29,000 miles on it, with all the bells and whistles. That V-6 had some punch to it; a four-door with a sunroof. Sweet! I drove it home and was set to get $1,000 the next day. My wife tacitly approved. She said that when she first heard I had bought a new vehicle, she remembered a dream I had related to her a few years ago about driving a new red pickup truck. She could just see me parking a new red pickup truck in the driveway.

The next day I cleaned and washed her paid-off car and took her to the car dealer. They needed her car for the trade-in on my new red pickup truck. And I forgot to tell her. Anyway, it got me an additional $2,000 cash in my pocket just before Christmas! She was upset. She refused to get out of the car. She saw the truck sitting by the door at the dealership. Things were not looking good, since I needed her signature or the payments would be $30.00 more per month. When you can't afford $480 per month, $510 doesn't help any!

So this is what I did. I told her that she had veto power over the deal, because I would not do it without her signature. This was sincere because I

still wanted her to be my wife. When she said
"No," I drove slowly out of the dealership lot. I
mentioned casually that we would be unable to
make the December house payment on both the first
and the second mortgages, and by the time we
reached the street, she was softening. I was getting
a little nervous. The salesmen at the dealership
could only guess how much trouble I was in.
Springing a new truck on a wife requires great
finesse (you try it sometime and see if you live to
talk about it!). Anyway, before we got to the other
driveway into the dealership, she said it was up to
me, so I turned slowly back into the packing lot and
parked the car. Now all I had to do was get her into
the pickup truck. I asked her if she would like to sit
in the new truck. She said tentatively, "ok." Then I
went into the dealership, signed my part of the
paperwork and took hers out to the car for her to
sign. I knew she would not go in. She was still
pretty upset. She signed the papers, looked
wistfully at her paid-off car, and said defiantly that
none of her money would be used to pay for the
new truck, to which stipulation I immediately
agreed. A small concession indeed, considering the
fact that our funds were irretrievably intermingled.
After we arrived home, she took possession of the
keys to the Grand Prix, purchased 4 days earlier,
and said it was her car. A done deal! And no
payments till February!

Now that more time has passed, she has
found that her new car is much nicer than her other

car, albeit, fully liened, and my new pickup with
only 30 miles on the odometer to start with has
provided us the capacity to haul things that really
needed to be hauled, like two new mattresses for the
children for Christmas. This difficult memory will
lighten up in time, especially once the cars are paid
for, unless we lose our house again.

One Year Later

CHAPTER 7

HOUSEKEEPING AND COOKING

I did not marry my wife to be a live-in maid, dishwasher or cook. I married her to be my wife and queen. That made me a husband and a king. It works nicely that way. However, somebody had to clean the house and plan meals, so while she was having babies, that became my opportunity to make her life happier. Often women have long periods of fatigue and depression during the early baby years. I could also mention that they sometimes assume an entirely new persona from the one they had on their wedding day. Over time these anomalies may correct themselves without intervention. In other words, ignore a lot of this stuff and hope it goes away! Meanwhile, wash dishes, do laundry and clean the house as much as you can while trying to earn a living and don't forget to fix dinner, or bring home Chinese or KFC.

In extreme conditions, I recommend a rake in the family room with the trash can close by. Don't worry about the toys, because if they are important ones, the kids will go looking for them later outside in the trash can. Meals can be simple yet nutritious, such as spaghetti, home-made pizza, potato soup (my favorite!), and chicken with rice and BBQ sauce in the oven at 375 for 1 hour in a covered pan and 6 cups of water (feeds 10). Throw in a can of green beans and it's a complete meal. Our children learned to hate powered milk. But none of them died.

Hopefully you will become good at multi-tasking and have a dishwasher. We didn't for many years. I had to use rubber gloves because I developed a skin condition. Laundry can be washed and dried between other tasks, but folding and putting it away has always been over the top. The pile on the sofa or in the middle of the floor just kept getting bigger.

Do the best you can without complaining and your wife will love you forever. Eventually the children will all move out and you will have a clean house. But beware of grandchildren!

CHAPTER 8

DOS AND DON'TS

Here is a quick list of good ideas and bad ideas:

DOS:

1. Write her poetry.

Poetry is good stuff. It can be better than flowers. In our family, my wife is the poet and has written many poems. There is a reason why Browning and Shakespeare did so well. I wrote a few lines of poetry early on, but none in over twenty years, until I wrote this book. (See page 57) Iambic pentameter can be really effective. You get big points for just trying.

2. Take her on a date once a week without children.

We tried everything. Nursing babies need their mother and sometimes teenagers need to be treated special, so dates with children can be good too. I did not take her on a date for a year or two and it was not good.

3. Open the car door for her.

We got out of this habit over the years, to my shame. Recently I took her on a date and parked at the Cineplex. We were early so we talked for a few minutes and another vehicle, a company service truck, pulled in next to us. I could barely see the passenger, who looked like a woman. She just sat there until her husband came around and opened the door for her and gave her a nice long kiss.

After witnessing such a wise husband's excellent technique, albeit more out of shame than spontaneous armoire', I rose to the occasion, opened my wife's door to help her out and gave her the most sincere kiss I could muster. I had nothing to brag about that day.

4. Take out the trash.

This can be assigned to the children, but the ultimate responsibility must be shouldered by the man of the house. This includes pulling the garbage can out to the curb. I did not marry my wife for her to be in charge of the garbage!

<u>5. Say a blessing on the food and lead in family prayer</u>.

Every religion has some form of family worship and blessing on the food. This is a tradition that children relate to and gain faith from. Do everything you can to strengthen relationships through church and community activities.

<u>6. Whenever possible, attend family reunions, gatherings, and funerals</u>.

Contact with your extended family is very important. A daughter marries a man, but a man marries a family. I missed my grandmother's funeral and regret it to this day. She died while I was stationed in the Navy in Europe. I have applied that lesson in life by attending all the other funerals of close relatives. It has paid rich dividends in personal reconciliation.

<u>7. Help her develop her talents</u>.

After about ten years of marriage, my wife became interested in oil painting. I bought her an easel, brushes, canvas and oil paints. She read books and learned on her own with great results. She has painted on saw blades and reproduced a favorite painting for her brother. She loves to paint and it makes her very happy to have that talent in her life.

8. Don't worry about finding your soul-mate; just make your chosen wife into your soul-mate.

I married my soul-mate (because I made her my soul mate!), the woman of my dreams, the queen of my castle, the mother of my posterity, the love of my life. The terminology of a "soul-mate" is a recent invention but the concept goes back to Adam and Eve. We may yet discover that the wives we marry here in this life were brought into our lives by a higher power more directly involved than we ever thought possible.

9. Build family traditions with your children.

We have had family nights, family plays, family contests, and music (i.e., a piano, trumpet, trombone, drums, and violin) in our home throughout the years. My wife and I with various children have participated in church choirs. Because of our interest in education, my wife and I have a huge library with a wide variety of books. All of our children grew up avid readers of both fiction and non-fiction. Each child had his or her own Bible. We lived on our ranch over 7 years with little access to TV but we had lots of movies and videos, including many of the classics. At Christmas, we re-enacted the story of the birth of Jesus, usually with one of our boys as the Virgin Mary, and the youngest as the baby Jesus. I was the donkey most years. Our daughter originally was casted as the baby Jesus but later advanced to be the Virgin Mary.

10. Take dance lessons.

Early in our marriage we took weekly dance lessons to learn the waltz and other simple steps. It became our weekly date and even though it lasted only a few months, we never forget it and we love to dance every chance we get.

11. Make her laugh.

Joy and happiness can be engendered by leaving things on her pillow (after making the bed), giving her compliments on her personal appearance and accomplishments, saying nice things about her in the presence of others, and using terms of endearment. Special names for each other expressing the sacredness of your love can be "secret" yet the children will hear those words or see them on birthday cards and know that mom and dad really love each other.

12. Make her your best friend.

The more you confide in her and make her the central part of your deepest heartfelt feelings, the happier she will be. She will consider you to be her best friend, the one person in the world she can trust and depend on no matter what. Confessing mistakes and faults to her will only deepen the relationship. Be the first to say "I'm sorry" and the last to accuse. Sometimes we all need a hug.

13. Look at the stars together.

On summer nights, when we lived out in the country, we would take blankets and pillows out on the trampoline and look at the stars. The children would fall asleep and need to be carried in, but the night sky was always inspiring. This is hard to do in the city, but camping trips make star-gazing possible. Learn about the constellations and some of the ancient legends. It is a real connection to the collective past of mankind.

14. Ask for help when you know your marriage is in trouble.

Twice in our marriage we went to the dreaded marriage counseling. It really wasn't all that bad. My wife suggested it and to humor her I went along. I did not think we needed any help. However, I found out that I was not listening to her growing concerns about our relationship. She needed someone else to tell me to wake up and pay more attention to her and her needs. I quickly agreed to listen better and take her on a date once a week, whether she needed it or not. I discovered that she really appreciated my willingness to change and to make her needs a higher priority in my life. I learned to listen better and to do more things with her. We have played tennis together, ridden bicycles, and gone on walks in the evening. We had a pass to a swimming pool at a hotel for a year so we could go swimming several times a week at an indoor pool. The hot tub was nice too. There are lots of ways to improve a boring marriage and bring new life into a relationship. Don't wait until it is too late. Make a bad marriage good and a good marriage great!

DON'TS:

1. NEVER MENTION WEIGHT or the word "FAT". (This topic is death!)

2. NEVER MENTION HOUSEWORK OR CLEANING.

3. NEVER LOOK AT PORNO.

4. DON'T FLIRT WITH OTHER WOMEN.

5. DON'T SWEAR. (You can know all the words, just don't use them!)

6. WHEN TALKING TO OTHER WOMEN, NEVER SAY ANYTHING ABOUT THEM BEING PREGNANT.

7. DON'T GET JEALOUS. (When she gets jealous, say "Hey! You really do love me!)

8. DON'T TAPE RECORD HER SNORING TO WIN THE ARGUMENT.

I hope these are no-brainers, but sometimes I am on autopilot and bad things can happen. If you need any of these explained to you, there is no hope. I should mention that the "how do I look" question is a trap and must be tip-toed across every time she uses it. You will have to test the wind direction, her mood, the seriousness of the tone of the question, the barometer for atmospheric pressure and take your best shot. Humor might work, but lying is usually better, if you can guess right on which way to lie. Personally, I like ambiguity. It doesn't always work, but it buys time to come up with an acceptable answer. I have even tried the truth, but it is very risky. You're on your own on this one.

Obviously this is not an exhaustive list, but these are the big ones. To make your woman happy is a lot easier if you stay out of trouble!

CONCLUSION

I cannot say that I have always made my wife happy over the last 30 plus years of blissful marriage. She has been disappointed in me and for those moments I am truly sorry. However, on the whole, like a well-built ship that rights itself after capsizing, when things come back to an even keel, all we have to do is a little clean up and everything is fine. The happy memories come back and the sky is blue and the wind fair. This is why the beginning is so important. Without a plethora of happy memories, beginning with courting, there won't be a strong enough foundation to build upon. Sadly our modern society is rife with divorce and sad memories. We must replace this pattern with longevity in marriages and happy memories. Our children need happy memories of their parents "in love." They will pattern their lives after ours.

When the storms of life hit, it is better to turn into the wind and face the big waves head on, with your wife by your side, and remember that *success in the home can compensate for any other failure!*

Truly, I Do

You said I did not love you,
When you said goodbye.
You said I did not love you,
But I started to cry.

You said I did not love you,
As tears streamed down my face.
You said I did not love you,
To put me in my place.

You said I did not love you,
But you know I really do.
I proved it by my sudden tears,
And when I said "I Do!"

But I'm sorry that I hurt you,
More than words can ever tell.
I will love you forever,
In Heaven or in Hell.

So won't you please forgive me?
You know I've forgiven you!
For saying I don't love you,
When you know truly, I do!

By C.W. Hyzer, Sr.

APPENDIX

A LIST OF MY JOBS

Fuller Brush salesman
Dishwasher – Hospital Cafeteria
US NAVY – Petty Officer CTT-3; Top Secret
   Clearance; DD 214 USS Conway
Cannery Worker
Plastics Factory Worker
Janitor
Law Clerk
Sunday School Teacher
Lawyer
Lay Minister
Workers Compensation Claims Adjuster
Tax Collector
Social Security Disability Claims Examiner
Informal Hearings Officer, Department of Health
Collection Agency Owner
Truck Driver; tankers, fuel, acid, caustic, hay, steel,
   dry goods
Warehouse Worker
Truck Terminal Manager
Gold Miner
Writer

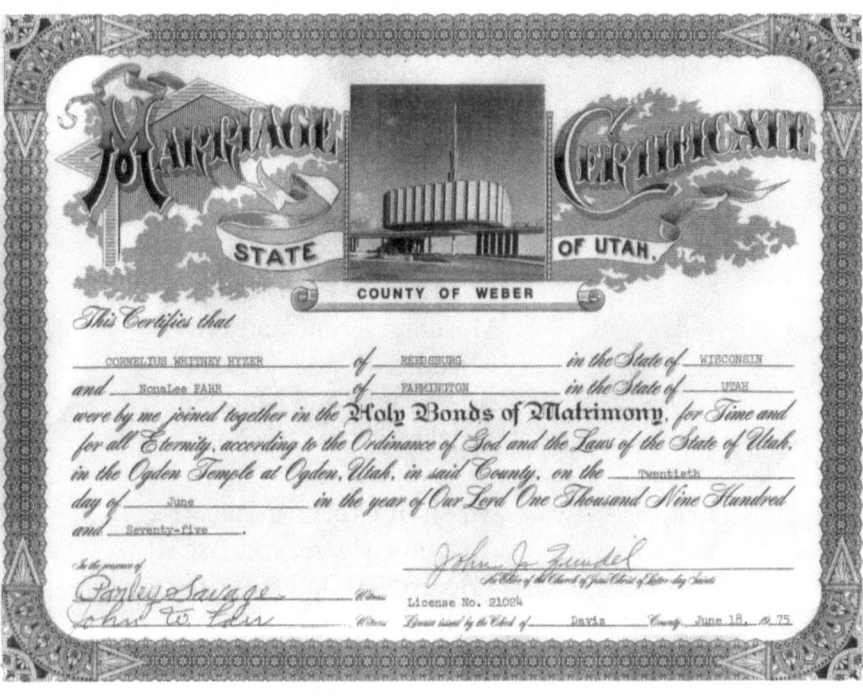

This Certifies that

CORNELIUS WHITNEY NYZER   of   REEDSBURG   in the State of   WISCONSIN

and   NonaLee FARR   of   FARMINGTON   in the State of   UTAH

were by me joined together in the *Holy Bonds of Matrimony*, for Time and for all Eternity, according to the Ordinance of God and the Laws of the State of Utah, in the Ogden Temple at Ogden, Utah, in said County, on the _____ Twentieth day of _____ June _____ in the year of Our Lord One Thousand Nine Hundred and _____ Seventy-five _____.

In the presence of

Parley Savage

John W. Farr

John J. Zundel

License No. 21024

License issued by the Clerk of _____ Davis _____ County, June 18, 19 75

In a Cowboy's Thoughts

By Nona Hyzer

Sagebrush, Rock and Blizzard
Scorchin' Desert heat
Windin' Mountain Trails,
Rattler at my feet.

Wire, Post and Nail,
Mendin' Fence 'fore Dawn.
Campfire warm and Friendly,
Sky goes on and on.

Mustang, Bronc and Filly,
Saddle, Rope and Boot.
Cattle Brands and Mavericks,
Learnin' how to shoot.

Smell of Cracklin' Bacon,
Biscuits, Beans and Beef.
Bedrolls round the Fire,
Tales of Cowboy Grief.

Ghosts and Gold and Holdups,
Courage, Fame and Guns.
Robbers, Hideouts, Legends,
Outlaws on the run.

Gunfights, Sheriffs, Lynchin's,
Lawless Western Towns,
Homemade wooden Crosses,
Pounded in the Ground.

BEAR IN THE MOUNTAINS

Oil painting on saw blade by Nona Hyzer

When You Were There

In the beginning, when you were there,
And kneeling at God's feet,
You gave a solemn vow,
That on this earth we'd meet.

Then one last time we walked through the stars,
You whispered low yet firm,
That you would go first and pave the way,
I would follow in turn.

Trusting in your faith and in your word,
I let you go ahead,
Knowing I would follow in your steps,
And to your side be led.

The way was long and hard and clouded,
I wandered here and there,
Giving, taking, wondering, praying,
And almost in despair.

With confusion swirling in my mind,
I was swept to and fro,
A sweet kiss here, a soft word there,
Give up to him? Oh No!

A promise rang through the star swept night,
A whisper low yet firm,
Love, I'll go first and pave the way,
Please follow me in turn.

A faith in the promise that you gave,
Broke through the veil of earth,
I knew you were here, yet where to seek,
Was knowledge lost at birth!

So I waited knowing you would come,
By your word being led,
And then in God's house with binding vows,
We two would then be wed.

Then you came as I knew you would,
One day in early fall,
You were different; I didn't know you.
Me, you didn't recall.

Still there was something deep in your eyes,
That drew me to your side,
And soon our love was reawakened,
Yes! I would be your bride!

But the way was not clear for us,
Just one more test of love,
To serve the Lord with all our hearts,
To work for Him above.

So now one more promise has been made,
But faith will ease the pain,
I know without doubt you'll hold me soon,
We'll never part again!

A covenant, a vow will bind us,
Forever we will be,
Husband and wife in infinite love,
For all eternity.

And together we will walk the starts,
Yes, hand in hand we'll say,
We've done this once before my love,
Oh bless that happy day!

NonaLee Hyzer

LIST OF PICTURES

ABOUT THE AUTHOR

Cornelius W. Hyzer, also known as Neal Hyzer, was born in Wisconsin and received his B.A. in History from the University of Wisconsin – Madison, after serving in the U.S. Navy. He graduated from Marquette Law School and practiced law over 10 years. After moving west, he became a truck driver and a gold miner. He and his wife have had eight children, together with over twenty grandchildren, so far, and currently reside in the state of Wisconsin.

[AUTHOR'S NOTE: The quote "Success in the home can compensate for any other failure," was inspired by the famous quote of David O. McKay (1873-1970), 9th President of the Church of Jesus Christ of Latter-day Saints, "No other success can compensate for failure in the home."]